Sanchez Ventura

Simon Collings

Leafe Press

Published by Leafe Press
Nottingham, England.
www.leafepresspoetry.com

Text copyright © Simon Collings, 2021. All rights reserved.

Artwork copyright © Zoë Rubens, 2021. All rights reserved.

ISBN: 978-1-9999451-6-9

Sanchez Ventura

I should like to make even the most ordinary spectator feel that he is not living in the best of all possible worlds.

Luis Buñuel

C was browsing the shelves of a second-hand bookshop, searching for something out of the ordinary to read. He pulled down a copy of a slim novel, the work of a Latin American writer whose name he did not recognise. The book was called *In the Shadow of Dreams*. As he examined the cover the light in the shop grew brighter, and he became aware that his linen suit was crumpled and his shoes scuffed and coated with dust. The scent of gardenias briefly filled his nostrils. C opened the book at random and began reading.

Teresa woke, disturbed by the clatter of hooves in the street and the sound of voices. She got out of bed and pulled back the edge of the curtain. From her third-floor window she could see a group of young gauchos parading in the road, waving their boleros and whooping. One of them glanced up at her, then they galloped off down the street and disappeared into the night. The leader of the gauchos was called Sanchez Ventura. He walked with a limp. Since cattle ranching had become unprofitable they had taken to appearing in the dreams of people more prosperous than themselves. The number of riders in the group varied according to Sanchez Ventura's whim. Tonight they would bivouac in the shelter of a forlorn hope of restitution.

In a late-night café across the street a young woman sat in a pool of yellow light cutting out words and phrases from a pile of magazines with a pair of nail scissors. The only other customers were two men playing cards. The one to the left had a clay pipe in his mouth. Both were wearing hats. They were an exact likeness of the two figures in Cézanne's *Les joueurs de cartes*. The woman applied herself methodically to her task and soon amassed a large pile of excised text. This she scooped up and deposited in the waste bin by the door. Aki, the owner of the café, would later recover these fragments and compose them into brief, incoherent dialogues which he pasted into an exercise book. He imagined them one day forming part of an interminable graphic novel about the enduring appeal of Arthurian romance. The main protagonist of this putative epic was Sanchez Ventura, a used-car salesman.

After the gauchos had galloped off, Teresa returned to her bed. Unable to sleep she picked up the book she had been reading. The title on the cover was: *Guinevere's Room*. Someone had snipped out random words and phrases, leaving behind a curiously limping narrative, though one not without a certain whimsical humour. Teresa could not decide whether the missing words had been suppressed or set free by whoever made these cuts, and with the concentration required to construe the dismembered syntax she was soon asleep. In her dream she was walking down an empty street, a shower of words falling like confetti. She gathered some of the scraps that stuck to her dress and arranged them on the back of her hand, wondering if this might be a message. 'thus to express/ the texture of the past as/ a backlist of/ impossibilities,' she read.

As a youth growing up in Finland, Aki had wanted to be a rock star, but notoriety had eluded him. He wandered around Europe for several years, doing occasional work to pay his way. One summer, serving in a bar in Crete, he had the sudden realisation that regularity speeds up the passage of time and that repetition is the enemy of eternity. He packed in his job and began to live his life according to endlessly changing patterns, such as varying the times at which he ate or slept, his schedule governed by a daily consulting of the *I Ching*. Nothing need be open or shut within the borders of a porous futurity, he decided. In time he became increasingly delirious with fatigue so that everything seemed an illusion. Time moved so slowly that small details preoccupied him for hours, like the hard 'o' and sibilant 's' sounds of the word 'concupiscence'. He had always thought of himself as 'deep' but now when he tried to look beneath the surface he found there wasn't even a surface.

Coming out of the library Teresa was nearly trampled by a herd of wildebeest thundering past. A stranger seized her arm at the last moment, pulling her back onto the pavement. The man removed a clay pipe from his mouth. 'The work of fifth columnists,' he said, seeming to address the people passing rather than her. *'Agents provocateurs.* However much they try to cover their arses, when the shit hits the fan a faecal stench lingers in the breeze.' As he moved away from her he froze in mid-step, half turned, and looked back at her intently. His gaze seemed to challenge her to declare what she saw, what she thought she was looking at, who she thought she was. The bearded face reminded her of the painter Cézanne. He showed no sign of moving so she left him there at the roadside, arrested in mid-step, his eyebrows slightly raised.

The young woman with the magazines and scissors arrived at Aki's café between 9.00 and 9.30 on those nights when she came, and she generally stayed until midnight. She wore a voluminous yellow coat in all weathers, sandals or boots according to the season, and a navy-blue beret on days with an 'n' in the name. On her first visit she had explained to Aki that she planned to visit the café at that time most days and that she would like him to vary what he served her from the list of items on the menu, a bacon sandwich and tea one evening, a plain omelette with a glass of milk the next. He wondered how she had divined that he was the kind of man to accede readily to such an arrangement, but she did not encourage conversation and he did not ask. He had learned that it was better to be slipshod than to walk on eggshells. The pattern of her visits seemed to be determined by some kind of random process, the secret of which he could not guess.

A series of minor earth tremors shook the city. No one could remember such a thing happening before. Teresa could still see the evidence of the shocks on the street, hairline fractures in the dust, conversation consuming itself on the lips of strangers, the forlorn wail of a fog horn with only two of its letters changed. The authorities blamed the seismic activity on a mysterious herd of wildebeest recently seen terrorising the city. The tremors stirred long forgotten memories in the population, like nutrients in a lake, leading to rapid hair growth, embarrassing slips of the tongue, and recurrent bouts of melancholy. Sales of depilatories surged. Could the tremors be connected to the young gauchos Teresa had seen from her window? She had her own ideas, which she kept to herself, and about which we therefore know absolutely nothing. Waiting on the platform at the train station, the woman in the yellow coat noticed a man in a crumpled linen suit watching her through two holes he had cut in his newspaper.

In middle age Aki still adhered to some of his theories about temporal flows and the iniquity of orderliness. Behind the counter in the café he had stencilled a line from Baudelaire: '*Une oasis d'horreur dans un désert d'ennui!*' '*Le désert n'est pas hostile ni indifférent, c'est au-delà de ça,*' said one of the card players one day, removing his pipe as he did so. In the café window Aki had arranged a display of fairy lights, with different-coloured bulbs which flashed on and off according to a random pattern programmed not to repeat for a hundred years. Added to this he changed the colour of some of the bulbs each week, using a cipher of his own devising and a copy of Mrs Beaton's *Book of Household Management*. The spare bulbs he kept on a shelf under the counter, along with a page from a notebook on which he had written: 'A barrier as incitement exploits the elasticity of subjective time.'

Four gauchos wearing boleros sat around a table playing cards. A television was on in the corner of the room. 'So, Cathy', the presenter was saying, 'let's take off your blindfold and let you see what you've been eating.' 'The knave of hearts,' one of the gauchos said, laying down a card. The others groaned and threw in their hands. 'The first dish you tried was this.' The presenter passed the woman a tin from which she read: 'Traditional Irish stew, Irish style stew with mutton and vegetables.' 'You said you thought this was underwhelming.' 'Yes, I found this disappointing, just not enough flavour. I wouldn't buy it.' The gauchos paid no attention to the television. The dealer gathered in the cards and reshuffled the pack. 'And the option you much preferred…was this.' 'Happy life dog food,' she read. The audience roared with laughter. 'I kid you not Cathy,' the presenter said, putting an arm round her shoulder. Cathy started to sob.

Anton was a regular customer at the café. He had a dotted line tattooed around his neck along with the words 'cut here'. According to Anton a shadowy and amorphous group called THEY, authors of a vast body of folk wisdom and urban myth, exercised an unshakeable control over the daily lives of the city's inhabitants. 'Mysterious agents move within us,' he said, 'an invisible army oiling the cogs and wheels of the social machine.' From Anton Aki learned that random words had been deleted from official circulars and posters pinned on the noticeboard at the public library. A copy of Edmund Burke's *Reflections on the Revolution in France* had also been defaced. There was a brief item about it in the local paper which Anton left with Aki. Later, when the woman in the yellow coat arrived, the café owner casually placed the paper on her table, open at the page with the story about the library. An organisation calling itself 'The Word Liberation Front' had claimed responsibility. After she'd left he noticed she had cut out the words 'word' and 'words' each time they appeared in the article.

Lost for

Posters on a library noticeboard were defaced yesterday by an unknown person cutting out certain   and phrases with scissors. Later the same day one of the library's books was found to have been similarly damaged. The two incidents are thought to be connected. The removed appear to have been selected at random and the whereabouts of the missing text is a mystery. A group calling itself The   Liberation Front has claimed responsibility.

Mistaken identity

Police constable Leonard Dines was awarded £15,000 compensation by a tribunal yesterday after it was found he had been wrongly arrested and charged with impersonating a police officer. PC Dines was on duty at the time of his arrest.

After leaving the café the woman in the yellow coat walked to a nearby bus stop. The city had been enveloped by a thick fog and she could barely find the stop. The lights of some kind of vehicle moving in her direction became visible and out of the fog the shape of a bus emerged, an ancient model which no longer operated on these routes. The bus stopped and the woman got on. A group of party goers in fancy dress occupied the rear seats but the bus was otherwise empty. The woman took a seat near the driver, a Bengali man who began to sing an elaborate ghazal. The passengers at the back were dressed as wildebeest, and were talking excitedly in a language she didn't recognise. The fog became increasingly opaque until it turned into a dust storm. The bus seemed to make less and less progress, its wheels slipping in the accumulating drifts of sand. The driver continued singing and the woman slept, lulled by the gentle intransigence of the storm.

The room into which Teresa had been shown by the young man had a mural covering all four of its walls. From the style it looked as though it had been painted in the 1930s. Two elegant chairs and a small glass table, placed on a rug in the middle of the room, were the only furniture. She felt too nervous to sit, so remained standing and looked at the painting. The mural depicted a sub-tropical garden, full of flowering trees and shrubs. A couple were walking arm in arm along a winding path through the trees, a yellow bird perched just above their heads. On the wall through which Teresa had entered the artist had traced a colourful display of bromeliads. She paced around the room, pausing occasionally before the mural. One of the details which held her attention was a small building half hidden by foliage. As Teresa gazed at this she realised that the door of the building was an actual door, the handle a cleverly disguised *trompe l'oeil*.

Graffiti employing the texts excised from the volume of Burke had begun to appear on bus stops and walls across the city. The quote 'a thousand uses suggest themselves to a contriving mind' had been pasted across the window of an empty shop. Stickers bearing the words 'prejudice is of ready application in the emergency' and 'some obscure and almost latent causes' had been plastered on lampposts and vending machines. A large poster reading 'destined to travel in the obscure walk of laborious life' had been fixed to the side of the Job Centre. Some of the graffiti appeared in people's dreams, and was reported by them on social media. The enlarging and pasting of the texts was believed to be the work of a group of gauchos operating on the frontier between slumber and waking.

Teresa tried the door and found that it opened into a kind of store room, at the end of which was seated a life-size waxwork of Sanchez Ventura, the man she had come to interview. He was dressed in a 1930s-style linen suit and seated at an escritoire, bent over an open notebook with a pen in his hand. His shoes she noticed were scuffed and covered in dust. Teresa closed the door behind her. A pale light fell through a single window on the opposite wall. A faint odour of putrefaction, the source of which she could not identify, hung in the air. She approached the pensive figure behind the desk. Its brow was creased, the eyes unfocused as if the writer were struggling to express something he couldn't quite find the language for. On the page before him were the words: 'But this was only the interruption of an imaginary incursion, the elliptical swerve of the phrase bending towards its invisible object.'

Sunlight was slanting in through the bus windows when the woman in the yellow coat woke up. The driver had disappeared, as had the party goers. The bus was half buried in sand, but the passenger door was open and she alighted to find that someone had laid breakfast for her on a small table: a bacon sandwich, still warm, a thermos of coffee, and a glass of orange juice. Soon refreshed, she began to explore. A trail of footprints led away from the front of the bus, the depression caused by the left foot less marked than that of the right, as though the person walked with a limp. 'The knave of hearts,' she thought. The tracks led up a slope through scrub. At the top she found herself standing beneath a tall pine tree, farm buildings visible in the valley below, a viaduct away to the right, a view of Mont Sainte-Victoire in the distance.

The sound of voices alerted Teresa to the arrival of people in the reception room into which she had first been shown. What would the great man think if he found her in the secret closet? 'She's not here,' one of the voices said. 'She must have noticed the door,' said another. Clearly there was no time to lose before they discovered her. She forced up the sash of the window and clambered out into a narrow alleyway. Just below the window lay the decomposing carcass of a small dog, very like one her family had owned when she was a child. It was covered with iridescent flies. But she had no time to linger. She ran down the alley, which was littered with small fragments of paper, to emerge into a busy city street. Across the road was a small cinema and Teresa decided to take refuge there.

One of the two films being shown was about to start. It was called *In the Shadow of Dreams*. A woman in a yellow coat, switching into the present tense for reason she alone understands, slips into an aisle seat towards the rear. There are only a handful of other people in the movie theatre. On the screen a woman is browsing the shelves of a second-hand bookshop. Piazzolla's *Libertango* is playing on the soundtrack. She takes a book from the shelf, opens it mid-way through. We see her rummaging in her bag as though searching for something. The scene cuts to a close up of the book, in which small sections of text have been carefully cut from the pages. The woman's right hand enters the frame holding a slip of paper on which are printed the words 'removed his clay pipe'.

Notes

Rafael Sánchez Ventura was a friend of Luis Buñuel. He worked as an assistant to Buñuel during the filming of *Las Hurdes* in 1933. The fictional character in this story has no connection with the historical Sánchez Ventura.

The line from Baudelaire appears in his poem *'Le Voyage'* and might be rendered in English as: 'An oasis of horror in a dessert of tedium.'

The comment in French by the card player translates as: 'The desert is neither hostile nor indifferent, it is beyond that.'

The phrases cut from magazines and used by Aki in this graphic novel come from the following sources: *New Scientist* 23 July 2016, *Cosmopolitan* August 2016, *Radio Times* 30 July–5 August 2016, *Autocar* 27 July 2016.

The quotations from Edmund Burke can be found on the following pages of *Reflections on the Revolution in France*, edited by Conor Cruise O'Brien, Penguin, 1969:

> 'destined to travel in the obscure walk of laborious life', p.124
> 'some obscure and almost latent causes', p.152
> 'prejudice is of ready application in the emergency', p.183
> 'a thousand uses suggest themselves to a contriving mind', p. 268

www.ingramcontent.com/pod-product-compliance
Lightning Source LLC
Chambersburg PA
CBHW071805040426
42446CB00012B/2714